WELCOME TO
THE UPCYCLED TOYS CLUB
A FAMILY FRIENDLY RECYCLING ACTIVITY SERIES

Dear Dalia & Ami —

Keep on being creative and always remember to use your imaginations!

By

Matt Duncan, MAEd

Illustrated by

Jonathan Rambinintsoa

Printed in the United States of America

First Printing, 2016

Download your FREE

THE UPCYCLED TOYS CLUB
A FAMILY FRIENDLY RECYCLING ACTIVITY SERIES

Bonus Items!

Get a PDF Upcycled Toys Club Coloring Book

AND

Special Edition Toy Instructions!

Visit

UpcycledToys.Club/FreeColoringBook

DEDICATION

This book is dedicated to:

The trees who were turned into cardboard boxes,
The dinosaurs who were turned into plastic,
The recycled materials that will get used to make something new,
And all of the wonderful minds which will be forever changed by the lessons in this book.

Yosef, Aviva, and Elijah, whose upcycling story inspired this upcycling story.

And of course Brianna, whose wisdom and inspiration made everything possible.

Welcome to The Upcycled Toys Club

Welcome to The Upcycled Toys Club, the first interactive coloring and activity book of its kind! Designed for both parents and children, The Upcycled Toys Club generates an experience that the entire family can enjoy. This upcycling activity book provides an easy-to-use guide intended to spark your child's creativity by allowing parents and children to work together to create new toys, utilizing resources that are free, easily obtained, and readily available in your home. Most likely, you already have everything you'll need!

As a parent, purchasing toys can become expensive, especially for children with expansive imaginations and rapid child growth and development. By utilizing the activities in The Upcycled Toys Club, you can help to alleviate this problem by constructing toys with your children; toys they can personalize and play with time and time again.

While there are various ways in which we can contribute to modern conservation practices, influencing your child to take part in working to reduce our carbon footprint is an important step toward a cleaner future. By completing these crafts with your child using recycled materials, families can introduce the concept of sustainability early on, reducing household waste and helping to maintain environmental wellness. Instead of constantly throwing away and replacing toys made of plastic, The Upcycled Toys Club will help save money and provide instructions to help you and your family make your own. Not only that, but all of these projects can be used as add-ons to the toys your child already has, such as the Car Garage project. With a little bit of ingenuity and some creative elbow grease, you and your child can complete projects that reduce the amount of resources taking up space in your house or local landfill.

Don't worry if you aren't a crafty person, that's okay! You don't need to be an expert to build these toys for your child. Even if it doesn't come out looking perfect, your family will have spent time engineering and decorating their own built-to-fit toy. Each activity is measured using a five star system indicating it's difficulty level. This way, parents can determine which toy constructions work best with their children. If you are working on our coloring book activities with an older child, then The Upcycled Toys Club coloring activities are the perfect opportunity to develop and practice their fine motor skills, such as learning how to use scissors, glue, and follow instructions to assemble things.

Please join The Upcycled Toys Club Facebook page at facebook.com/UpcycledToysClub/. On our page, you will have the opportunity to share your projects with other people in the community. When your family has completed all of the toys, we'd love to hear about you and your child's experience with The Upcycled Toys Club! Read about other successful stories from other parents and enjoy a collaborative space where families can discuss their creative projects, explore new projects, and amp up the imagination. If you've enjoyed this coloring book, then we welcome you to visit our website at www.upcycledtoys.club and sign up for the Club, so you can get instructions to build all of Evan's toys!

How It Works

Before you begin to work on the activities included in The Upcycled Toys Club, parents and their families are encouraged to read and follow the information provided below to help keep projects easy, fun, and safe.

As you start getting ready to create the projects in this book, you should begin to gather, collect, and save the following household supplies and store them for when your child wishes to start on a new toy.

- Cardboard boxes and pieces in various shapes and sizes.
- Pizza Boxes
- Toilet & Paper Towel Tubes
- Clear Plastic Paper Protectors
- Old CDs
- Plastic Container & Tops
- Detergent Caps
- Liquid Body Wash Pop Tops

While we pride ourselves on designing projects primarily constructed using recycled household materials, this activity series requires all of the following tools in order to be completed:

- Scissors
- Box Cutter
- Tape
- Glue
- Hot Glue & Hot Glue Gun
- Brass Paper Fasteners
- Decorating Materials (Markers, Stickers, etc.)
- Thin Rope or String

Do your best to the follow the instructions and feel free to change it to suit your own needs! Add in your own designs and enjoy hours of enjoyment, building and playing with your toys. Make sure to have enough paper and ink before printing off our exciting activities.

An Important Note About Adult Supervision

Parents or another adult <u>must</u> be present and supervising during the construction process of all Upcycled Toys Club activities! Many of the tools required to put together these toys are not appropriate for child use. <u>DO NOT</u> allow young children to use box cutters, hot glue guns, or cut thick cardboard, as there is a serious risk of injury involved to small hands. Please be sure to use common sense to ensure that nobody gets hurt. We are not responsible for injuries that occur while you are creating the toys in this book.

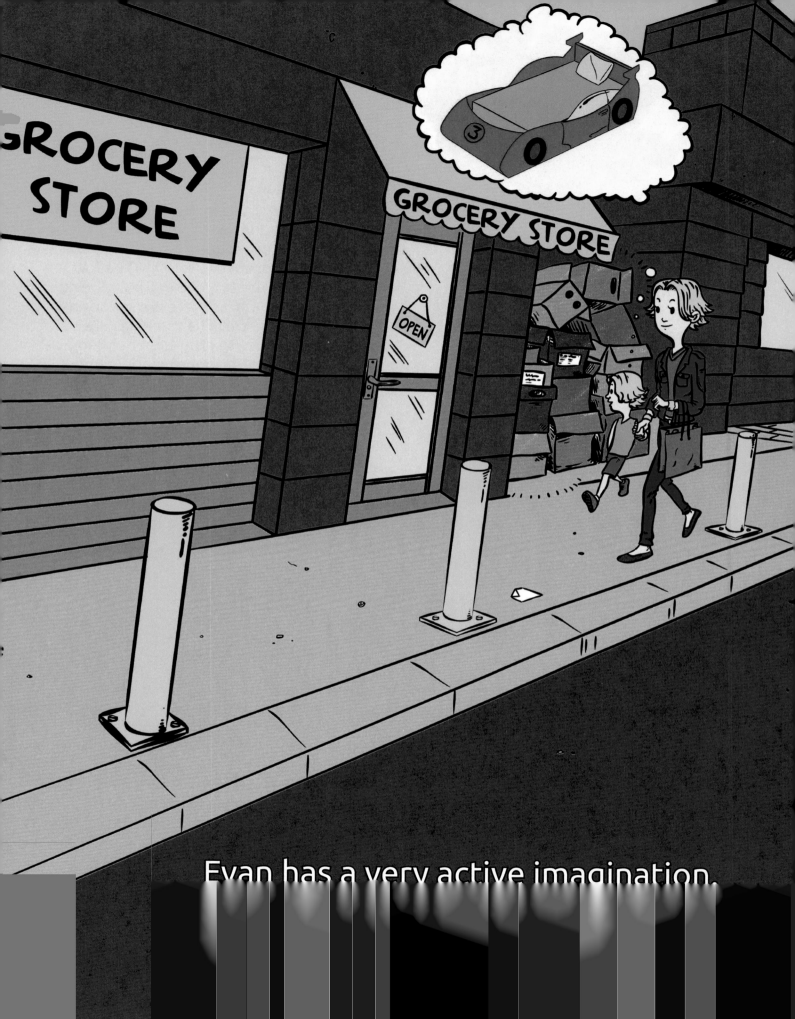

Evan has a very active imagination.

Evan's imagination is always lighting up with ideas about what he can upcycle with all the things that he sees others throwing away. This happens wherever he goes.

It all started with a visit to Aunt Brenda and Uncle Mark's house. When Evan arrived, his cousin Claire showed him her new play kitchen that the family had made together by upcycling old cardboard boxes.

Evan could not believe how much fun he had playing in his cousin's make-believe kitchen.

Evan and Claire played all day in the kitchen as they pretended to cook their favorite dishes. They even threw a tea party for all of their toy animals.

As soon as Evan got home, he immediately set to work designing his own toys. First, he built a shelf on which to put all of the things he was going to make.

Then he made a lap-desk so that he could sit on the couch and draw his designs to use the cardboard boxes his family had in the garage.

Evan had a full week of activities coming up, and he was very excited to make toys from cardboard with his friends and family!

Evan called his Uncle Mark, who gave him some great advice about how to organize his supplies to start making more upcycled toys.

Following Uncle Mark's advice, Evan and his family set to work organizing all of the materials in the garage into an Upcycling Corner. Evan decided he was going to create a new club, called *The Upcycled Toys Club*, so he could share upcycling with all of his friends and family.

When Evan came up with a new idea for a project, he and his mom would write out a list of the things he would need on his whiteboard, and collect into one box all of the materials that they would use for that project. This way, whenever it was time to make the project, everything he needed was in one place.

Once Evan knew what he needed for each project, it was easy to organize everything and save materials. Sarah even helped him to go through the recycling bin and take out all of the things they needed for the next week's building projects.

Whenever he saw anyone in his family about to throw away something, Evan would be sure to ask them to save it. He always made sure to carefully wash out anything that had food in it so that it wouldn't get yucky.

When Evan's grandpa got to his house, he had a stack of boxes under each arm.

Evan, his grandpa, and his dad set to work turning Evan's bed into the race car bed he'd always dreamed of having.

Evan had so much fun building the race car bed that he wanted to share upcycling with everyone he knew!

The next day was Monday. Evan and his dad decided that he needed a parking garage for all of his toy cars. So they built one from a pizza box.

Sarah was very excited to join them and play with the cars. Her favorite part was sending them down the ramp that they built together.

On Tuesday, Claire and her friends Shane and Josh came over to Evan's house. They built a castle and suits of armor for Sir Evan and Sir Josh, the knights. Sir Evan rode on his horse to protect the castle from Shane the dragon, who was trying to get inside it.

On Wednesday, Dylan and Nick came to play with Evan. He took them on an adventure where they sailed in their pirate ship across the seven seas.

After reaching the island, Evan, Dylan, and Nick started to dig. Soon they found a chest of buried treasure. I wonder what's inside of it?

On Thursday, Evan decided to fly to Mars. He made a fabulous spacesuit that anyone traveling into space must wear. Then he built himself an interstellar spacecraft.

Even though Evan left Earth all by himself, he met
a new friend, Marvin the robot. And guess what?
Someone had made him out of cardboard!

Friday was Evan's birthday. All of his friends came to celebrate with him. They were so surprised to see that all of the games at his birthday party were made from... you guessed it ... cardboard!

Everybody's favorite activity was the puppet theatre that turned into a photo booth after the show. Everyone piled in and said "CHEESE!" to get their pictures taken.

Saturday was the day of the big community block party. Evan, Chase and Kayla decided they were going to put on a concert with instruments they made themselves. Before the show, they put everything together and got it ready.

When it was their turn to take the stage, Evan sang and played the guitar, Kayla was on the keyboard and Chase rocked out on the drums.

Sunday was a big day for Evan. His mom got a text message from Nick and Dylan's mom. They had decided to have a safari and build their OWN toys!

Evan's mom showed him the picture of Nick and Dylan driving their cardboard car around the backyard, while their sister Marcy flew around in her airplane and spied on them with her binoculars.

Evan was so excited that his friends had started to build their own toys that he went back to his drawing board to start designing the next week's projects. I wonder what he will come up with next.

DISCUSSION QUESTIONS

★ Describe some ways that Evan was creative?
★ Why is creativity important?
★ Who would you like to share your creativity with?

★ What materials did you see Evan and his friends use to make toys in the book? Do you use these things in your house?
★ What materials do you have in your house that you could use to make a new toy?
★ How can using things you already have to make new toys be good for your family? How can it be good for the Earth?

★ Which of Evans toys was your favorite?
★ What do you need to make that toy?
★ What things will you need to save to make that toy?

★ Why did uncle Mark tell Evan to make an upcycling corner?
★ Why is it important to keep our supplies clean and tidy?

★ Why is it important to protect the resources we have?
★ Can you name some precious resources?
★ Where does a cardboard box come from? Can you trace it back to the seed of a tree?

★ What is a landfill? What happens to things when they go to a landfill?
★ Can you explain why it is important to keep things from going to the landfill?

★ How would you describe "upcycling" to your friends?
★ How is upcycling different than recycling? How are they the same?

WELCOME TO
THE UPCYCLED TOYS CLUB
A FAMILY FRIENDLY RECYCLING ACTIVITY SERIES

Are you ready to join The Upcycled Toys Club and make your own toys, just like Evan and his friends?

Turn the page to find out how to make 10 of Evan's toys! Can you find each of them in this book?

To learn how to make all of Evan's toys, join the club at www.UpcycledToys.Club

Safety Reminder

Always remember that cutting thick cardboard can be difficult, and that box cutters,
scissors, and other tools can be <u>very</u> sharp!

Hot glue can be dangerous, as it gets <u>very</u>
hot!

Always remember that a responsible adult
should be present whenever using tools
that can hurt you!

As much fun as it can be to build new toys,
always remember...

SAFETY FIRST!

THE UPCYCLED TOYS CLUB

A FAMILY FRIENDLY RECYCLING ACTIVITY SERIES

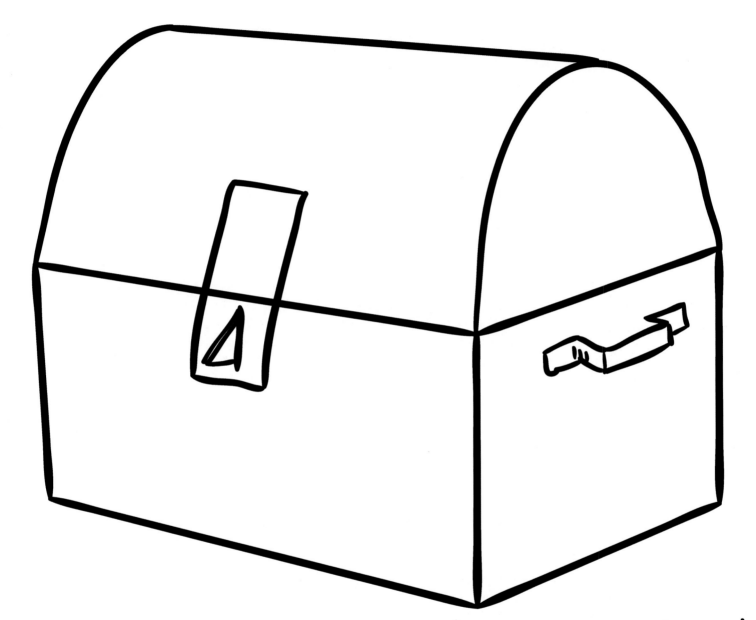

Create your own upcycled treasure chest!

Difficulty	Approximate Time Required
***	60 Minutes

1. Place one box on top of the other with the open ends faced inward. Using a marker, outline the rounded top of your treasure chest onto both sides of the cardboard box. Cut along the lines with the box cutter.

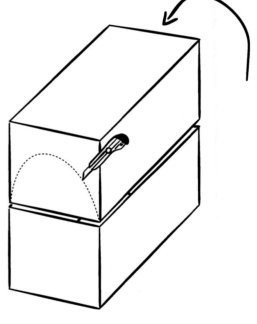

2. Cut away the remaining pieces of each side from the top of your treasure chest and place them aside. Take the leftover cardboard to form the top of your treasure chest. Use hot glue to secure the 2 rounded pieces in place.

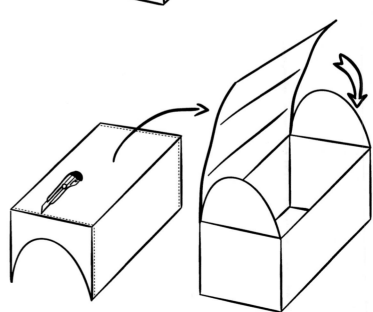

3. Use tape alongside the back of your treasure chest to form a hinge. Make sure to reinforce it from the inside! Glue the rest of your pieces together as desired.

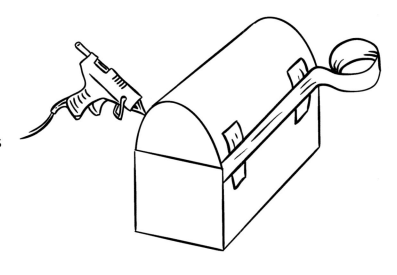

4. Using the pieces of leftover cardboard, cut out 2 even strips and fold them into the handles for the treasure chest. Check to make sure the handles are spaced equally on both sides before gluing everything into place.

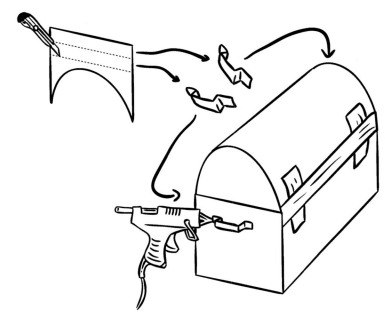

5. Taking the final piece of cardboard you have left, outline the desired lock for the treasure chest. Using a box cutter, cut out the top piece of your lock and make a slit. Attach it to the top of your treasure chest using glue. Glue together the remaining cardboard pieces to form the bottom section of your lock. Secure it to the bottom half of your chest. Make sure they align!

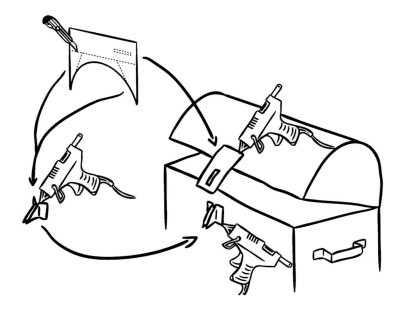

6. You're all done! This is going to be the perfect place to hide all of the treasures found during future adventures. Keep your booty safe!

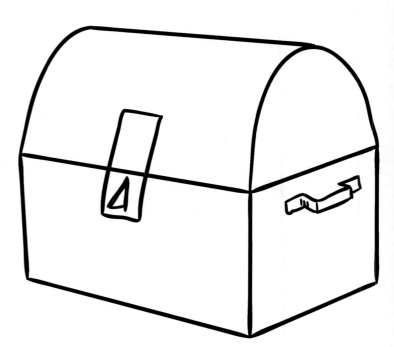

THE UPCYCLED TOYS CLUB

A FAMILY FRIENDLY RECYCLING ACTIVITY SERIES

Create your own upcycled microphone!

Difficulty	Approximate Time Required
*	20 Minutes

Things You'll Need:
- A kitchen sponge
- A toilet paper tube
- Black spray paint
- Scissors
- Hot glue

1. Using scissors, cut the sponge into a ball and place it on top of the toilet paper tube.

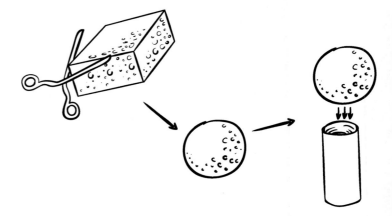

2. Glue the ball to the top of the tube.

3. Spray paint the entire ball and the tube black.

4. That's all! Pass the Mic, it's time to get on stage. What will you perform for the audience tonight? Sing, act, tell jokes, and make sure to have fun up there!

THE UPCYCLED TOYS CLUB

A FAMILY FRIENDLY RECYCLING ACTIVITY SERIES

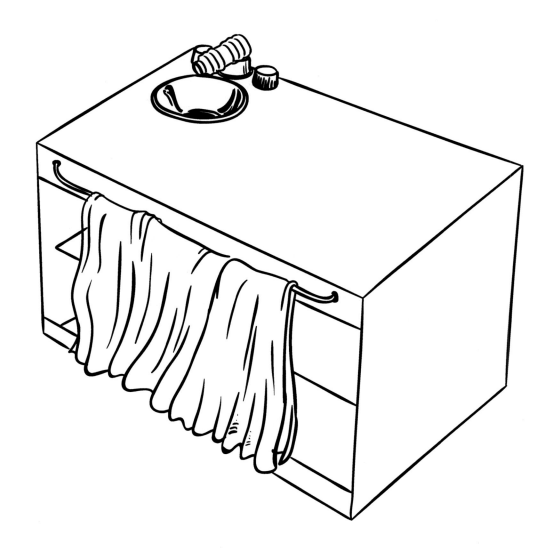

Create your own upcycled kitchen sink!

Difficulty	Approximate Time Required
+++++	15 Minutes

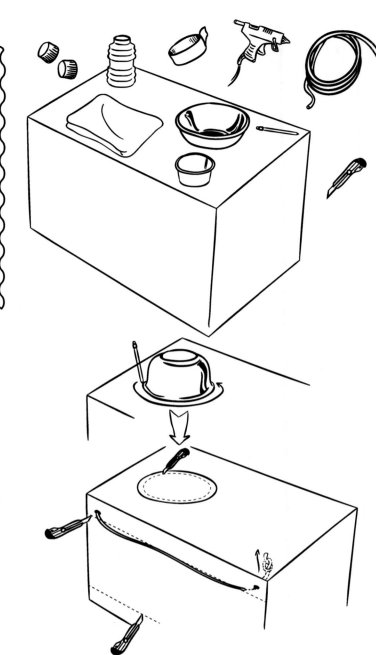

1. Trace the outline of the bowl on top of the cardboard box, then cut out a circle that is slightly smaller than the one you drew. This will keep the bowl of your sink from falling through. Next, use a box cutter to cut out the front panel of the cardboard box. Leave a couple of inches at the top and bottom to keep the box from collapsing. Make holes on both sides near the top edge of your sink, and hang the rope or thick string across the whole width of the box and secure into place by putting the string through the holes and tying a knot at each end.

2. Place the bowl into the hole to create the sink basin. Insert the piece of cardboard, previously cut from the front of the box, into the structure to create a shelf. Secure it into place using tape.

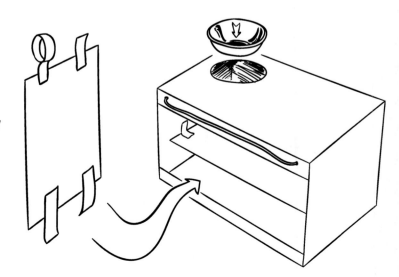

3. Use hot glue to secure the 2 laundry detergent caps into place to form sink handles, then put the yogurt cup, opening down, between the two caps to form the base of the faucet. Glue the plastic bottle to the top of the yogurt cup to complete the faucet.

4. Finally, hang the towel over the rope and cover the contents hidden underneath the sink.

5. You've completed all the steps! We're about to cook a family dinner. Time to wash up!

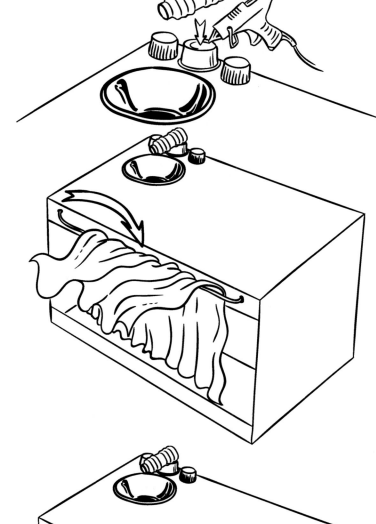

THE UPCYCLED TOYS CLUB

A FAMILY FRIENDLY RECYCLING ACTIVITY SERIES

Create your own upcycled car track!

Difficulty	Approximate Time Required
*	20 Minutes

Things You'll Need:
- As many pieces of cardboard that you'll need in order to create the desired length of the car track
- Tape
- Hot glue
- Painter's Masking Tape
- Markers, stickers, and other things to use for decoration

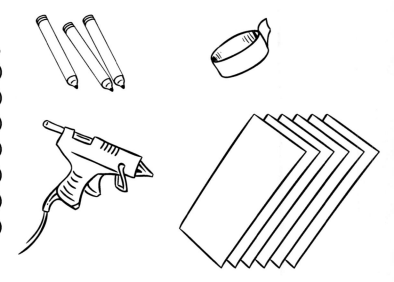

1. Begin by folding up the edges of the cardboard panels to make railings. This will prevent cars from driving off the track. Afterwards, glue each panel of cardboard together to make the ramp whatever length your child desires.

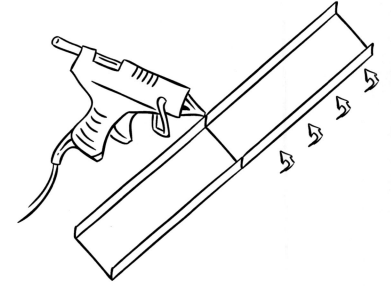

2. Choose a piece of furniture nearby a wall to help hold up the top section of the ramp. Using wall-friendly tape (such as painter's masking tape), secure the top of the ramp to the furniture and the side of the ramp down the wall.

WALL

Furniture as support

3. Optional: Use a piece of paper and markers to decorate a city scene to place next to your track. Get creative and make background scenes of your own!

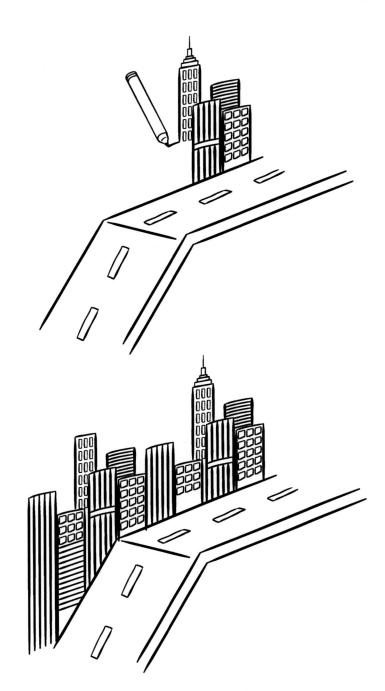

4. The ramp is complete! Which car do you think will drive down the track the fastest?

THE UPCYCLED TOYS CLUB

A FAMILY FRIENDLY RECYCLING ACTIVITY SERIES

Create your own upcycled crown!

Difficulty	Approximate Time Required
*	30 Minutes

Things You'll Need:
- A piece of cardboard with enough length to be folded in half
- A box cutter
- Markers, stickers, and other things to use for decoration

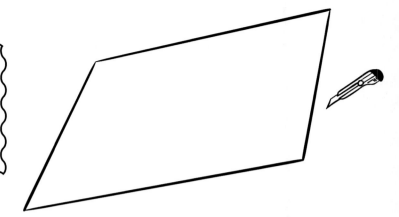

1. Fold the cardboard in half. Using a marker, outline the desired shape of your child's crown. Take care to make it large enough to fit around your child's head. Don't forget to make the etch seen in the diagram into <u>one side of the crown (not both).</u>

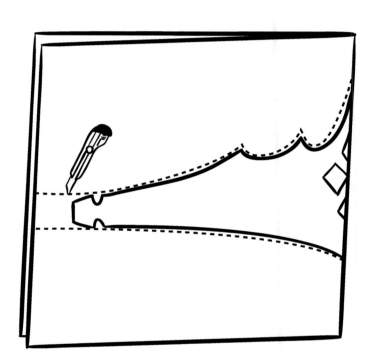

2. Carefully, use the box cutter to cut out your crown design. On the side, opposite of the etched flap, make a small fitted hole. This will help clasp the crown together when it's completed.

3. If the cardboard is corrugated, you can use the box cutter to separate the top layer from the corrugations. Now, your child can decorate and personalize it to their fancy!

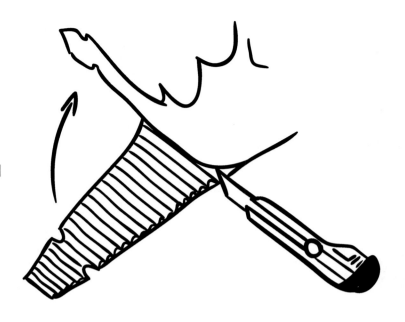

4. All finished! Time to join the royal family. Will you be a wise and gentle leader or an evil and villainous ruler?

THE UPCYCLED TOYS CLUB

A FAMILY FRIENDLY RECYCLING ACTIVITY SERIES

Create your own upcycled horse!

Difficulty	Approximate Time Required
****	45 Minutes

1. Place the 2 large pieces of cardboard together and make sure they are secured. Using the diagram as a reference tool, draw an outline of a horse head and mane using your marker across one side. Carefully, cut along the line with the box cutter. Cut a hole into the styrofoam big enough to fit the broom handle securely inside.

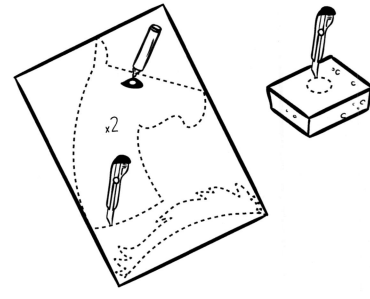

2. Using hot glue, attach the styrofoam to the middle of your horse's head. Cut out a small piece from the remaining cardboard. Fold the edges upwards and glue both sides to the bottom section of your horse's neck. Make sure to include a hole that aligns with the hole made in the styrofoam and pull your broomstick through. Finally, attach the other side of your horse's head down.

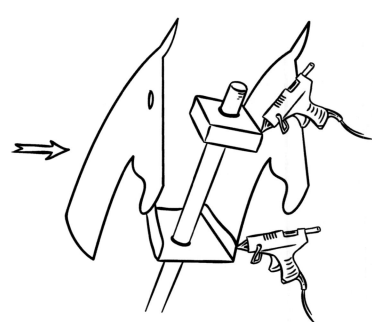

3. Take the long thin piece of cardboard and make sure it fits snuggly between both sides of your horse's head. Glue it down to keep it secure.

4. Take the mane and glue it firmly to the back of your horse's head.

5. That's all! Time to ride into the distance with your new companion and explore.

THE UPCYCLED TOYS CLUB

A FAMILY FRIENDLY RECYCLING ACTIVITY SERIES

Create your own upcycled space suit!

Difficulty	Approximate Time Required
*****	120 Minutes

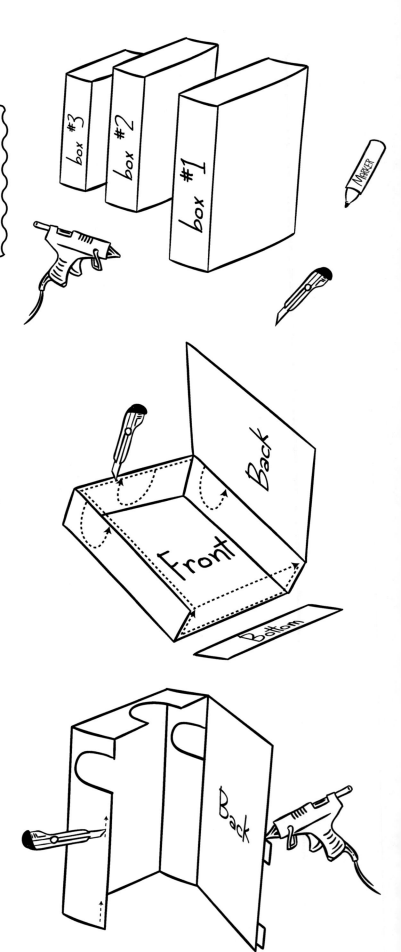

Things You'll Need For the Space Suit
- 3 rectangular boxes, each slightly smaller than the last
- Hot glue
- A box cutter
- Markers, stickers, and other things to use for decoration

1. Cut the edge of 3 sides of the back of one box, leaving the last side attached so that it can flap open and closed. Cut out the bottom edge, then cut out holes for the arms and head to fit.

2. Cut 2 small vertical holes along the open side of the box, then glue 2 tabs into the same position on the opposing edge of the suit's front flap. These will help to secure the suit closed.

3. Glue Box 3 and Box 2 to the back of the largest box. Box 2 should be glued to the back of your largest spacesuit piece.

4. Decorate the box to your own design with markers, stickers and other materials.

5. The body of your spacesuit is finished. Make sure you have a helmet or you won't be able to breathe while you travel through space!

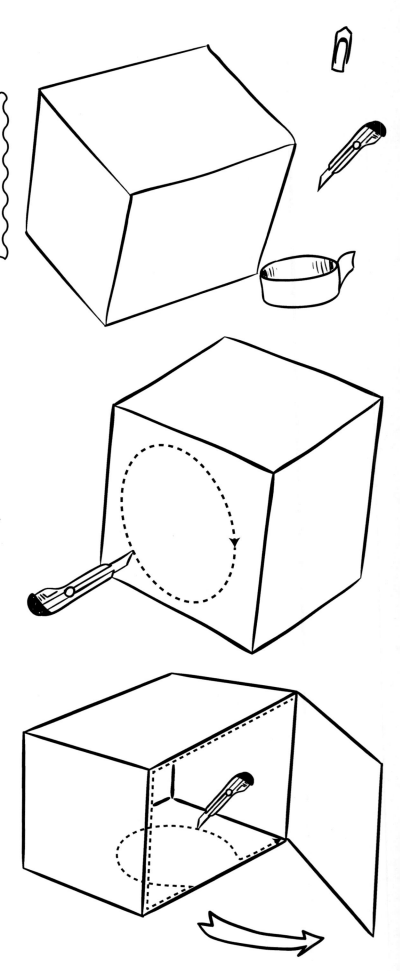

- A square box large enough to fit over your child's head
- A paper clip
- A box cutter
- Tape
- Markers, stickers, and other things to use for decoration

1. Cut and remove a large circle from the front of your box to create a hole that your child can see out of during their space exploration.

2. Cut 3 sides away from the back of the box leaving the fourth side attached, giving the helmet a way to open and close. Use the box cutter and cut out another circle from the bottom of the box. Make sure to extend the section of your circle out and into the side that faces the flap. Take care that it is large enough to fit around your child's neck.

3. Cut a small vertical hole along the side of the box where the open flap will close. Use glue to attach a small tab of cardboard to form a latch. This will keep the helmet securely shut in outer space.

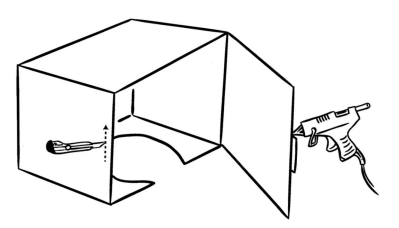

4. You're all finished! The helmet is ready for space travel! Houston? We've got contact!

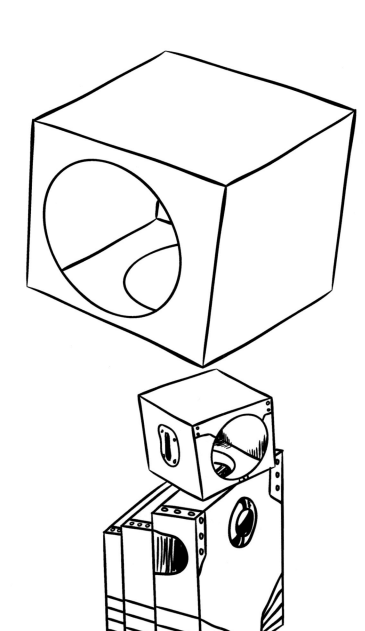

5. That's it! Your space suit is now ready to head out into the galaxy. Which planet do you want to see first?

THE UPCYCLED TOYS CLUB

A FAMILY FRIENDLY RECYCLING ACTIVITY SERIES

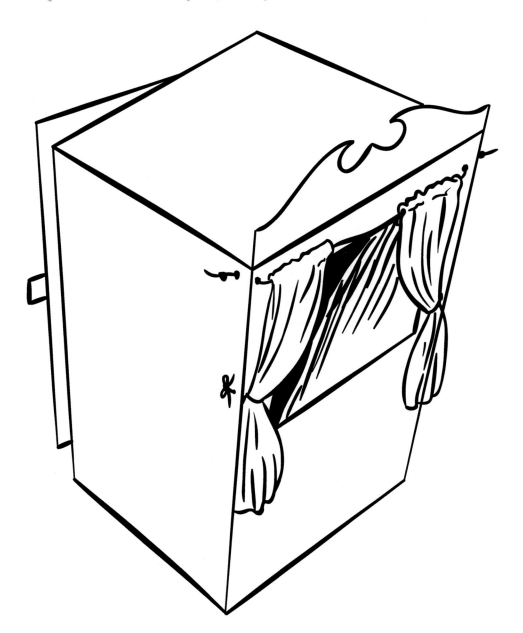

Create your own upcycled puppet theater!

Difficulty	Approximate Time Required
***	45 Minutes

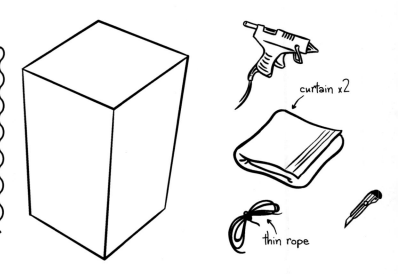

Things You'll Need:
- 1 large refrigerator box
- 2 pieces of cloth for the curtains
- A thin rope
- Hot glue
- A box cutter
- Markers, stickers, and other things to use for decoration

curtain x2

thin rope

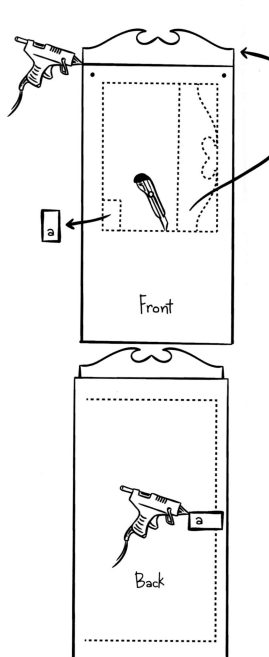

Front

Back

1. Use a marker to outline the pieces of your theater booth according to the diagram. The main window should start from the top and go a little more than halfway down. Use a box cutter and carefully cut out each piece. Take the piece that will serve as the top of your structure and bend the bottom edge. Use glue or tape to secure it into place.

2. Facing the back of the structure, use a box cutter to create a door. Make sure to keep the left side connected. Take piece A and glue it down onto the door to make a handle.

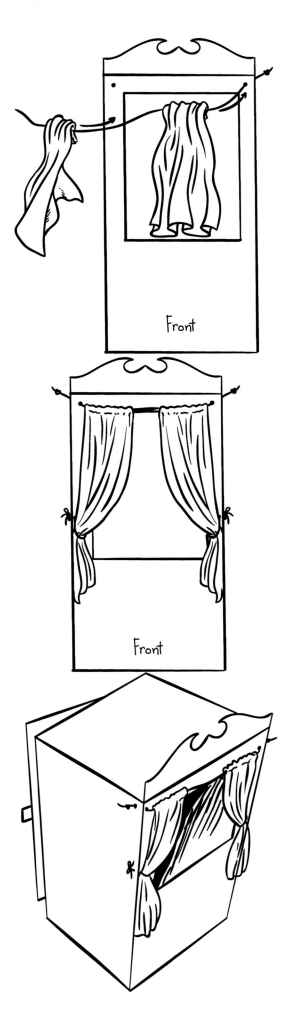

3. In the top section, above your window, make a hole on each side. Pull one end of the rope through one hole and tie a knot large enough to keep it secure. Place both curtains across the rope, then pull the end of the rope through the remaining hole. Tie it down in a knot large enough to keep the rope from being pulled through.

4. Make two more addition holes lower down on the box. Cut the remaining rope off and use it to tie the curtains back.

5. You're all done! What will be your first performance? Sock puppets? Hamlet? Ladies and gentlemen, the possibilities are endless.

THE UPCYCLED TOYS CLUB

A FAMILY FRIENDLY RECYCLING ACTIVITY SERIES

Create your own upcycled guitar!

Difficulty	Approximate Time Required
****	90 Minutes

Things You'll Need:
- 5 equally large rectangular pieces of cardboard
- Medium to large rubber bands
- Paper clips
- Wooden pegs
- Hot glue
- Power drill
- A box cutter
- Brass paper fastener
- Assorted bottle caps for knobs
- Markers, stickers, and other things to use for decoration

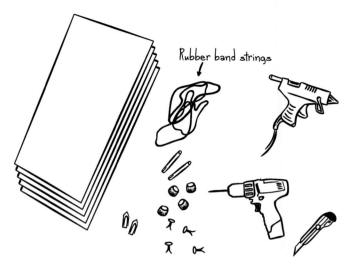

Rubber band strings

1. Using hot glue, secure 3 pieces of cardboard together to create a single thick, reinforced piece of cardboard.

2. Following the diagram, outline a guitar shape with a colored marker onto the top layer of cardboard. Use a box cutter to cut along the lines.

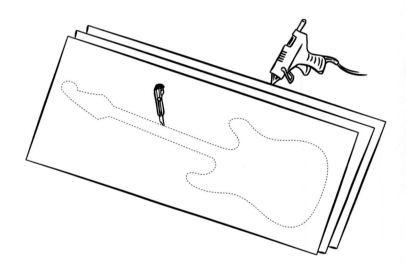

3. Take another piece of cardboard and outline the neck, bridge, and pick ups (decorative details) of the guitar. Use the final piece of cardboard to create a second shape of the body of the guitar. Carefully, cut each pair of pieces out and glue them together.

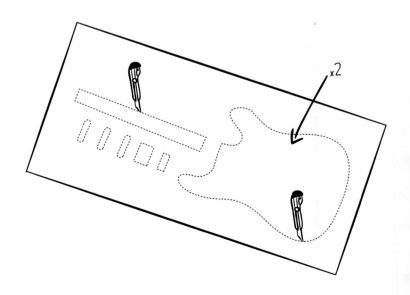

x2

4. Secure the decals and brackets of the last outline of your child's guitar with hot glue. Make sure to keep everything aligned.

5. Carefully, drill holes into the top of your soda bottle caps and use the brass paper fasteners to secure them into sound dials. They should be able to turn freely. Use a box cutter to form notches for guitar strings into one of the small wooden rods and glue it into place.

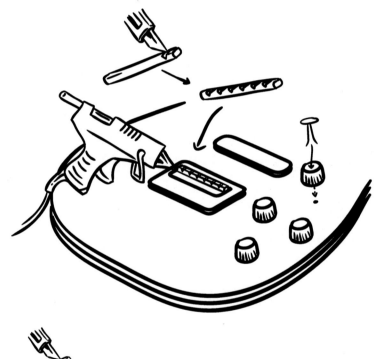

6. Make the same etches onto the other wooden rod, then glue it to the top of the guitar's neck to form another bridge piece.

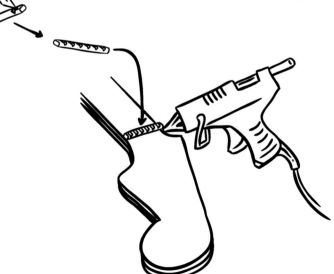

7. Use a power drill to form holes behind the first bridge. Make enough holes for the amount of strings you want on the guitar.

8. Drill the same number of holes into the neck of the guitar behind the other notched bracket.

9. Pull the strings of the guitar through the holes behind the first wooden rod, then pull them over the wooden rod and tie them to the back of the guitar. Finally, take the remaining two layers and glue them over the elastic band strings in the back for complete coverage and reinforcement.

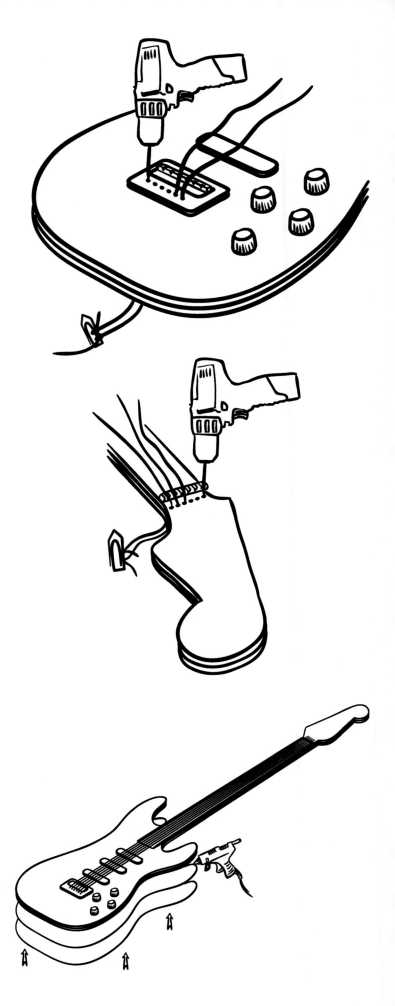

10. Alrightttt!!!!! Are you ready to rock n' roll? Grab your friends, make some more instruments, and start a band!

THE UPCYCLED TOYS CLUB

A FAMILY FRIENDLY RECYCLING ACTIVITY SERIES

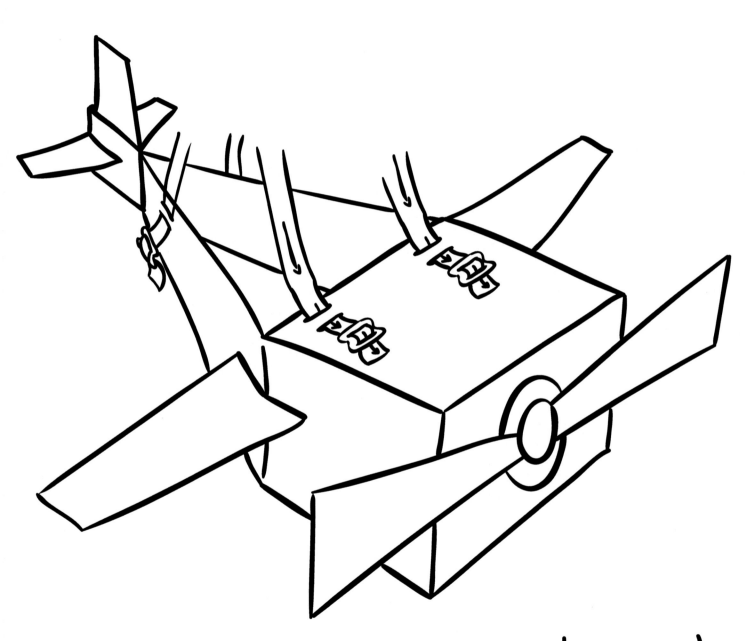

Create your own upcycled plane!

Difficulty	Approximate Time Required
✱✱✱✱	60 Minutes

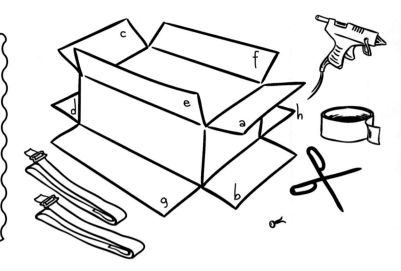

Things You'll Need:
- A large cardboard box
- Scissors
- Tape
- A brass paper fastener
- Rope, string, or any material for a strap
- Strap clips
- Markers, stickers, and other things to use for decoration

1. Cut off the flaps labeled B through H in the previous diagram. Leave flap A intact.

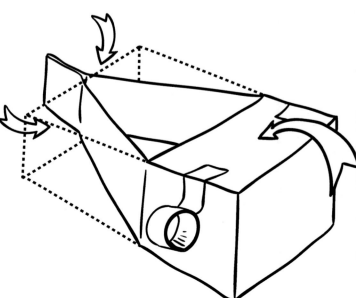

2. Use tape to secure flap A to the box, then fold the sides of the back of the box together to form the tail of the plane. Use tape to hold it in place.

3. Cut the remaining flaps (pieces B through H) into shapes to make the other parts of your child's plane. Pieces B and D make up the tail. Pieces E and H make up the wings. Pieces F and G will serve as the propellers. Following the diagram, cut piece C into parts to help hold the propeller together.

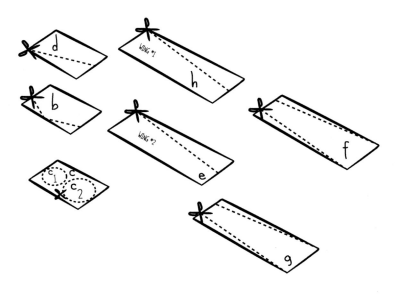

4. Cut a gap in the tail of the plane just wide enough for piece B to fit inside, then attach piece D to the top and complete the tail. Cut similar gaps into both sides of the box and insert pieces C and H into these gaps to make the wings of the plane.

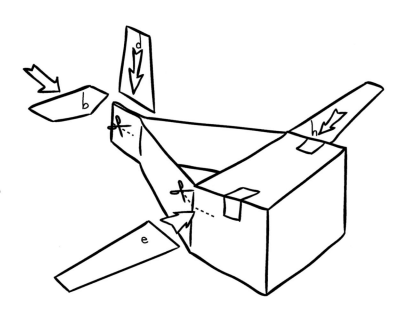

5. Glue the propeller pieces F and G to the larger circle that was previously cut from piece C, then glue the smaller circle over the propellers to secure everything into place. Make a hole in the center of the propeller assembly for the brass paper fastener, then punch a similar hole in the front of the plane. Afterwards, use the brass paper fastener to attach the propeller assembly. It should be able to spin freely.

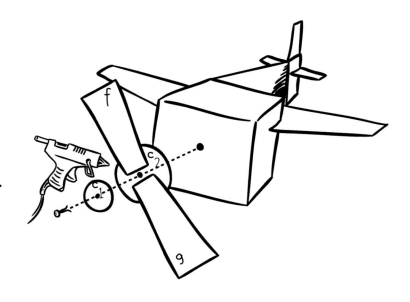

6. That's all! Time to perform a pre-flight check and prepare for take off!

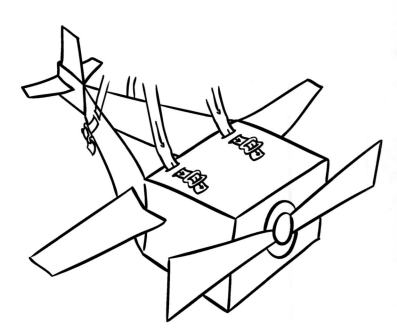

Thanks for being a part of

THE UPCYCLED TOYS CLUB
A FAMILY FRIENDLY RECYCLING ACTIVITY SERIES

We hope that you, your family, and your friends have had as much fun building toys as we have!

To find out more about The Upcycled Toys Club, and sign up for the club to receive new activities every month, visit us at:

www.UpcycledToys.Club

Be sure to join the Facebook community so that you can share the toys you've made, and ideas for new ones that you've come up with, by going to:

www.facebook.com/groups/upcycledtoysclub/

ABOUT THE AUTHOR

Matt Duncan, MAEd is an outdoor experiential educator, author, and entrepreneur whose focus is on teaching families the importance of protecting and preserving our environment. Along with his partner Brianna Greenspan, he co-founded Earth-Centric Innovations, a company which creates educational opportunities around green technologies that help to protect the planet. *The Upcycled Toys Club* is just one of the many ways ECI helps to teach awesome ways to make a positive impact on the world!

Matt's passion for the environment was sparked at a young age as a Boy Scout, and ever since he has always been fascinated by the wonders of nature, and is constantly on the lookout for new and innovative ways to instill the love of nature to his students.

Matt's other passions include camping, rock climbing, and any other activities that bring him closer to the Earth!

Matt was raised in Southern California, and now frequently travels to wherever adventure and nature's beauty lie!

ABOUT THE iLLUSTRATOR

Jonathan Rambinintsoa's passion for drawing was born the day he learned to put a pencil to paper. Ever since, his deep passion for drawing has continued to grow.

After being a web developer for 8 years, he decided to dedicate most of his time to his passion for art, and make it his career. Jonathan's exciting and innovative career is fueled by passion and an open mind.

Jonathan has spent the past several years focusing on his talents and career as a 2D artist, and every day becomes more passionate about his art, which motivates him to overcome the challenges of life, giving him the taste of endurance, hard work and success.

Jonathan lives in Antananarivo, Madagascar with his wife and children.

Made in the USA
Middletown, DE
15 January 2017